IMAGES OF REALITY

DOUGLAS W. HAPPY

authorHOUSE®

AuthorHouse™
1663 Liberty Drive
Bloomington, IN 47403
www.authorhouse.com
Phone: 1-800-839-8640

First published by AuthorHouse 11/10/2011

ISBN: 978-1-4520-8987-4 (sc)

Printed in the United States of America

This book is printed on acid-free paper.

For Mom
With all my love

Donna

Embrace the images
and define the reality

w/l

Doug

☺

ACKNOWLEDGEMENTS

First, I would like to thank my Dad, Charles Happy or better known as Chuck (RIP February 23, 2009). Thanks Dad for giving me the chance the last time I got out, which was the start of this exciting journey, in this new life. Without you, none of this would have ever been possible. I love you always and miss you, a hell of a lot.

Next, a special thanks to the Duluth area running community including Northern Minnesota Track Club, Austin Jarrow Sports, Grandma's Marathon and all the local running events and triathlons I have had the pleasure of participating in. Some of the friends I made: Bill Austin, Jarrow Wahman, Eugene and Barb Curnow Family, Don and Ella Fennessy, Dwane Anderson, Bill Barthen, Randy Back, Brian Patterson, Rod Raymond, Steve O, Lyle Koivisto and Joy Kops. You all made me a better runner and triathlete than I ever thought I could be.

I need to thank the all the teachers, writers and local poets who told me to keep writing, Ellie Schoenfeld, Patrick McKinnon, Liz Minnette, Al Hunter, Joseph Maiolo, Bob Monahan and especially my 10th grade reading teacher at Duluth Central 1973, Mrs. Anderson, who told me to write.

I need to acknowledge and thank those who believed in me, Reggie Walton, Gary Dosser and The Honorable John T. Oswald. To those in the courts, corrections and treatment centers, I did learn from you.

A special thought to those who suffer from the disease of addiction, and those who are no longer with us. Unfortunately, this list is too numerous and way too long. I miss you all.

Miigwitch, to the Great Spirit.

Finally, very special thanks to my editor, Becky Urbanski, Ed.D. Thank you so much for your patience and guidance.

LIFE

So far my life has ebbed away
I thought about it the other day

So many dreams and so much sorrow
Broken promises and unfulfilled tomorrows

It's a shame to suffer all the pain
Crying in darkness denying my bane

Reminded of hurting people in the past
I wonder and worry until I think at last

Is it them or is it I that has to change
To accept a life that doesn't seem so strange

First poem, spring 1974

ICE SKATING

I learned how to ice skate during the winter of 1969. After much convincing, my cousin, Lowell talked me into going with him. It was one of my most enjoyable, learning experiences. It was fun and not as hard as I thought it was going to be.

I thought back to when I went ice skating with my fifth grade class when we first moved to Duluth. We had made a quick, unexpected move during Christmas break when I was in the middle of fifth grade. I was a new kid, in a new school environment and felt completely out of place. I did not know a single person in that school. I was teased a lot and the target of bullies. I did not think I would be the only kid who did not how to ice skate. The other kids were excited and kept saying how much fun it was going to be.

Once we arrived at the skating rink, it was a disaster. My skates were too big, borrowed from an older cousin, and the kids were laughing at me already. I got my skates on and out on the ice in fairly decent fashion, but once I tried to skate I fell, and kept falling. The other kids were laughing, pointing at me and asking, "What's wrong, don't you know how to skate? Didn't they have ice skating where you came from? It's easy, you must be stupid and uncoordinated if you can't even skate," they said.

I felt like a complete idiot and fool.

Some of the aggressive kids who really had a problem with me knocked me down as they skated fast by me. Others made quick turns and quick stops right in front of me, spraying me with ice. I tried to get out of their way but my feet would start slipping faster and faster. 1 would end up falling every time. It became a game to see who could make me fall and get everyone to laugh. A few times I fell, hit my head on the ice and I saw stars. It really hurt and I wondered why I was even there. It did not take long for me to get off the ice and go inside. I sat all alone in the warming shack as everyone else was having fun, skating. One of the teachers came by and asked me what was wrong. I told him I couldn't skate.

"Oh well, don't worry about it, just have fun like everybody else," he said as he headed out on the ice. I couldn't tell him I was getting tired of knocked down and laughed at. I was the new kid and I did not want to cause any trouble. So I just stayed inside by myself for the rest of the time we were there.

Those were my memories of ice skating as I listened to my cousin, Lowell, trying to talk me into going skating with him. He assured me there were no other kids who were going to knock me down and laugh at me. He said there was a beginner's rink and the other kids who were going to be there were not that good of skaters themselves. Everyone fell down and laughed together. I was skeptical but I wanted to learn how to skate.

We arrived at the rink and watched as other kids skated by. I noticed the different skill levels right away. Some kids were pretty good at skating and others looked pretty shaky. I could see myself skating with these kids all right. Some were falling down, but the difference was that nobody was laughing at them. They were all laughing and having fun. Maybe skating would be fun after all.

Lowell instructed me through the whole process. He had the right size of skates for me and showed me how to tie them tight. That was one of the secrets, he said. We got on the ice and he showed me how to turn my foot, to push off and glide. I was able to take a few strides and glide along the ice. I was amazed, I could skate! Of course I fell and so did a lot of the other kids. It was a beginner's rink and everyone was trying to get the hang of it. We were all falling down, laughing and having fun. My biggest thrill was being able to glide down the ice at what seemed an incredibly fast speed and not fall. It was scary at times because I could not turn or stop. We made sure we skated off to the side so we would not run into people or be in their way. Lowell showed me one way to stop, by turning one skate sideways and drag it behind the other skate. I found a way that was much more fun. I would get up some speed and pile into a big, soft snow bank at the edge of the rink. A number of us kids had a contest to see who could fly the farthest and do the coolest wipeout. It was fun discovering the thrills only kids can come up with. Another trick was to try to see how fast I could get going before wiping out and go spinning and sliding down the ice. This seemed like a game everyone was trying. You could hear the laughter, screams and shouts all over the rink. It was fun to do and watch.

I did not realize how wet and tired I was until the walk back to my cousin's house. We only had to walk a couple of blocks but it felt longer.

"Didn't I tell you it was going to be fun?" Lowell said.

"It was great! I can hardly wait to go again," I exclaimed." Can we go tomorrow?"

"Sure," Lowell said," I told you it was going to be fun and you did not want to go at first."

"Yeah I know, I 'm glad we went," I said.

It was quite an adventure. We met some new friends who were learning to skate and some who were really good skaters. Lowell even knew a few kids who played hockey on a team. They must have been good ice skaters if they played on a team, I thought. Maybe some day I would be good enough to play hockey, perhaps good enough to even play on a team. I thought I was dreaming too big. I was just learning how to skate, but I loved it. Gliding down the ice at what seemed breakneck speed was so much fun. I wanted to learn everything and skate all night long. I thought how different it was from the first time I went ice skating.

SUMMER 1970

One day during the summer of 1970, my friends and I were playing together at the local schoolyard. On the field we were playing, there was a warming shack for the ice rink. Seven of us, ages 10 -12 were riding bikes, hanging out and hoping to get a baseball game going. A man around forty-some years old with a graying crew cut came up to the field from a nearby house. We could tell he was angry about something the way he stomped onto the field and his intimidating stance. He looked at me and said, "Who threw all those pieces of shingles and tarpaper from the warming shack into my yard?" "We just got here mister, we don't know what you're talking about," said Joe. We looked over the fence into his yard and saw shingles and tarpaper all over in the man's yard. I felt a cold shudder of warning and ice water flowed through my stomach. I felt a rush of fear and desperately wished I were somewhere else at that moment. If I were not sitting on my bike I probably would have taken off running. The man angrily shouted, "I want to know which one of you little bastards threw that garbage in my yard?" Everyone looked at him, then looked at me, because he was looking directly at me. "What the hell are you looking at me for?" I asked. His face registered shock as if I had just thrown a bucket of cold water on him. He took a couple of steps towards me. His face turned red as he clenched his fists. He spat out, "Listen here punk, you smart mouth me and I will rip you off that bike and kick your little, smart ass. You hear me, boy?" Our eyes were locked as I knew not to back down, but I was scared spit-less. I hoped I looked like I was glaring back. I replied evenly, "Yeah, I hear you, man."

I continued to stare directly at him and thought I was going to break;

but I could not look away. It seemed like an eternity but he finally turned and looked at the others. "I'm talking to all of you and I won't call the police if you go down there and pick up that mess!" he ordered. He looked at me again, and said, "I mean all of you." My friends immediately went down to his yard and started to pick up the pieces of shingles and tarpaper. Nobody said a word as they worked quickly. I slowly walked down to his yard but had no intention of picking anything up. We had not done it, so why should we pick it up was my rationale. To me, cleaning it up was just like admitting we had done it. I stood at the edge of his yard as the others scurried around picking things up. The guy briefly looked in my direction but looked away when he saw I was not helping. He seemed intent on instructing the others. They quickly had the mess picked up and we were heading back to our bikes.

The man said," Don't ever do that again and if you ever need to get a ball in my yard, that's okay. You have my permission." I thought, what a jerk. I hoped we would put a ball through his window. That would serve him right. We were back on our bikes in the field before anyone spoke up. One friend Randy said, "Doug, you're lucky; I thought for sure that guy was going to kick your ass." Chris said, "He sure didn't like you, Doug. Do you know him?" "Why was he only looking at Doug when he was talking?" Joe asked. My best friend, Jim, replied, "Because he's an Indian."

Everyone looked at me as I looked around, then back to Jim as he nodded his head. I looked around again and I could see some of them didn't get it. I looked at Jim and as our eyes met we both understood perfectly well what had happened.

Randy said, "I couldn't believe when you asked that guy 'why the hell are you looking at me?' I thought for sure he was going to knock the shit out of you."

Everyone nodded and agreed it was a brave and stupid thing to do. They asked me if I was scared and I told them, "Yes, of course, I was scared."

I also told them we didn't do it so why should we take the blame? I knew the guy was singling me out because I was Indian but I wasn't going to put up with his racism. I was mad because I was being blamed and he took it for granted I was the guilty party because I was an Indian. It seemed like I was always going to get it, no matter what. Afterward when Jim and

I were alone he said," Doug, don't ever do that again. I was scared and I thought that guy was going to really hurt you." I reassured him I would not do that again but I knew if the same circumstances happened, I would act the same way. I had to- it was my nature and sense for survival. If I backed down, I would be dishonoring my people. I would be dishonoring myself, too. I would take the risk of whatever happened, would happen. Any day is a good day to die.

FALL

September 1972, five friends and I decided to skip the last hour of school. It was the beginning of ninth grade for three of us, Chris, Steve and I. Bob, an eighth grader, joined us with Robert and Jim, two seventh graders. That previous summer, Duluth had experienced a torrential storm that flooded some streets. First Avenue West by Washington Jr. High School was washed out completely. Construction crews had the area blocked off and were installing new storm and sewer pipes. Since it was the start of the school year, we figured attendance could be explained away and left school. It was the perfect chance for a group of young boys to explore and have some fun. We all decided checking out the damage and devastation was more exciting than sitting in a hot, stuffy classroom. The avenue that washed out was across from the school going north, up the hill. We met after sixth hour and decided to go up First Avenue West to a playground up on Eighth Street. It was a secluded area away from the school and nobody would notice us, or so we thought.

We saw another group of kids from our grade that was skipping class, too. We figured a lot of kids were skipping class to survey the damage. Many kids were not from the neighborhood and wanted to see the damage everyone was talking about. It was a big deal for all of us and the other kids who heard about it. They all wanted to see what had happened.

Since it was my neighborhood, I had experienced the storm firsthand and was providing all the details. A creek that ran underground in a storm drain had washed out a portion of the hillside in Cascade Park and flowed down the avenue. Lightning had struck a manhole cover and blew up the underground culvert which the creek flowed through. It opened the creek to flow through the park causing extensive damage. The washed out area was about thirty feet across and around twenty feet deep. We made our way through the park and headed to the playground which was two more blocks up the hill beside the creek. We arrived at the playground, glad we made it without being caught and wondering if any school officials were going to find us. The guilt of skipping class combined with the thought of the assistant principal following after us made us nervous. We had snuck through the woods to get there and did not want to get caught at our destination. The playground had a partially enclosed slide known as a tornado slide. We played in this slide. It served as a hiding place as well as a lookout point. We had been there for about ten minutes and were thinking on moving across the street to a different area. Chris and I were at the top of the slide getting ready to go down. The others were already at the bottom. We heard someone talking and it sounded like grown up voices. We stayed hidden inside the slide. Steve said, "Come on down, some guys want to talk to us."

I had a bad feeling something was going to happen. We slid to the bottom and stood up. We saw two adults, one older guy I recognized and a younger, bigger guy who looked to be in his mid-thirties. The older man lived by Cascade Park and thought of himself as caretaker of the park. The neighborhood kids didn't like him. He was always threatening to call the police because he claimed we were wrecking everything, which we were not. It didn't matter, we were kids and he was the adult.

The younger man was carrying a long handled, socket bar which he held in a threatening manner. The old guy had a little crescent wrench in his hand.

"Yeah, that's him. He's one of 'em," said the big guy.

He looked directly at me.

Steve said, "This guy said, some kids threw his kid's toys in the ditch by his house down the street. His kid's started crying and said the big kids laughed and told them they were going to throw them down in the ditch, too."

We all said it was not us and did not know anything about it, or what they were talking about.

The big guy took a couple of steps toward me.

He said, "It was you! Don't lie to me, it was some goddamn Indians and you were there. I saw you!"

I said, "It wasn't me. I was with these guys the whole time."

The big guy yelled out, "Bullshit! We followed you. I heard my kid crying came out and saw you guys heading up the hill."

The old man agreed.

He said, "Ja, vee seen choo's coming up in dis' direction, unh vee followed chah. Ja, it vas choo". I protested again and said, "Yeah, we came up from down there but we didn't do anything, or even see any kids".

I was getting angry. "You shut your fucking mouth and don't lie to me you son of a bitch!" the big guy shouted. He pointed the socket bar at me and said, "It was you and keep your fucking mouth shut! I'm a truck driver. I'm not from around here and I'll hit you over the head and throw your body down in that ditch. You hear me, boy?" I nodded, not daring to say anything. "I don't like stinking Indians so you just give me a reason and I'll kill ya, I don't care," he said. I was so scared I could not move. I felt like I was standing on a bowling ball, trying to keep my balance. I could picture myself lying in that ravine; head bashed open, blood pouring out. I wished somebody would come by, some grown up, the police, the assistant principal, anybody. The big guy said, "You ever come near my place or my kids again I'll fucking kill ya. I'll come over to your fucking house while you're sleeping and I'll kill ya." "Let's get out of here before I change my mind," he said to the old guy. The old timer said, "Ja, choo's better lissen to him, vee know where you liff". Nobody said a word as the pair walked back to the creek and down the hill. They disappeared into the brush and I was shaking so bad I had to sit down. Steve asked, "You know those guys, Doug?" "I know the old guy, he lives by the park," I said. "I really thought that guy was going to kill me."

Bob said, "Yeah, that guy really wanted you, Doug. I thought he was going to kill you. I was getting ready to jump him from behind if he tried anything."

We all knew he was talking nonsense but it was a relief just to hear somebody speak. Steve asked, "Did you hear what he said about Indians? I wonder if he just said that or if there were really some Indians who messed with his kids?" I said," Who cares, that guy was an asshole and he's lucky I didn't have my baseball bat with me. In fact I'm going home and going to get it and pay him a visit. I think I know where he lives." "Never mind, Doug," Chris said. "That guy probably would kill you if you went after him." I said, "Yeah, probably, but I would still like a chance to meet up with him with my bat. Then I would like to see how tough he is." I was so angry I really thought about going after him. I knew nothing was going to happen, though. We were in the wrong by skipping school and what could we prove anyway? The only lesson was the reality of some redneck wanting to terrorize a young Indian kid.

BROKEN SPIRIT

Christmas Eve 1978 and it could not have been worse. Twenty years old, on probation, unemployed, no job skills, alcoholic and living in his parent's home looked to be a dim future. Hap Williams thought his life was over and at the lowest depths of despair anyone could ever imagine. Recovering from a severe beating those three guys had given him a few weeks earlier only added to the misery. It did not matter that they had set him up to drink alcohol with them and planned on jumping on him for any reason. The plain matter of the fact was - they did not like him. In truth, they hated him and wanted to hurt him bad, which they surely did. They waited until he was very intoxicated and made up a story to start a fight. They claimed he had said something about their mother, which he had not. They knocked him down and put the boots to him, kicked him numerous times in the head and face when he was down. He was in the hospital for a week with a broken nose, multiple contusions, fractured jaw and cheekbone.

His family and acquaintances said it was his own fault because he chose to drink with those guys. That was only another piece of a violent cycle in a long list of bad things that had happened to him

About a month and a half before, the police had picked him up for drunk, passed out in a hallway of a local hotel. This hotel was notorious for drinking, fights, stabbings, and other crimes. The police were not too happy about carrying a drunk down a few flights of stairs and more the less dragged and pushed him down the stairs. That was the start of cursing from Hap. After handcuffing him as tight as possible, they threw him down in the back of the squad car. One of the police officers was telling him to shut his mouth or he was going to get it shut. When the police dragged him out of the squad car, they were rather rough and Hap called them a few choice swear words. The one cop grabbed him by the arm and threw him face first into the side of the jail building, thus breaking his nose, knocking out two teeth and fracturing his cheekbone. The end result was a charge of disorderly conduct, resisting arrest and assault. Hap was sentenced to thirty days in jail or go to treatment for chemical dependency with a condition of a year's probation. Treatment seemed like the easiest option since he did not like the thought of sitting in jail.

In August a month earlier, a group had tried to rob and kill him in a park in Colorado. The group who attacked him started out drinking with Hap and figured they would rob him. The only reason he made it out of that one was he was not that drunk and was able to run away. But not before getting hit, kicked and threatened to have his eyes cut out with a knife. He had been in Colorado because he thought he could make a new start. A girlfriend had sweet- talked him into going there and made him promise he would not leave her. Hap did not leave her- she had left him.

So here he was back in his hometown on a cold, snowy Christmas Eve. He thought his parents and everybody blamed all his misfortunes on him, so what could be worse? An acquaintance stopped by and invited him out for a night of drinking. Tom had a car, was paying for the drinks, and it seemed like great way to escape a depressing Christmas Eve sitting all alone.

The night began well with a promise of being a good time. The first bar they stopped at had a good crowd out for a night of drinking and telling stories. Some old high school buddies Hap had not seen for a while were at the bar and having a good time. He could tell that by the laughter, smiling faces and good-natured kidding they greeted him with that night. The first question they asked was what had happened to him. Hap told them he had gotten in a fight. Their reply was, wow, they would have hated to be the other guy. The drinking and stories continued and Hap thought it was a good time. The evening went by fast, and soon it was closing time and everybody was heading home. Hap was pretty drunk and his drinking buddy, Tom, was drunk, too. They were in the car heading back home when a car passed by too close and the vehicles sideswiped each other. Hap, being the passenger, was the first one out to see what happened. What a mistake, the other car had five guys who were out for blood. They immediately started hitting and kicking Hap, calling him a dirty, fucking Indian.

"Tell your buddy to get out of the car, we're going to get him too, you fucking Indians", one of them said.

Tom who was in the car had seen enough and took off.

One guy said, "That's just like you fucking Indians, trouble starts and you fucking run. Well, we got you anyways and you're gonna pay." The biggest of the five continued to hit Hap. He tried to fight back but he was too drunk and there were five of them. He was outnumbered.

"Look what he did to the car, you fucking Indian", someone said. "Let's get that motherfucker." As soon as Hap started to fight back they all swarmed over him. He was knocked down, tried to curl up and cover his face.

The biggest guy said, "Don't cover up, ya fucking pussy, you're just gonna get it worse. Take it like a man, you fucking, dirty Indian cocksucker."

"Pull his hands away from his face, Joe," he said.

As soon as Joe pulled Hap's hands away from his face, the others kicked him in the face. This produced a flurry of kicks to the head and face from a number of the attackers. With every kick he received, Hap saw multiple explosions and stars. He started to pass out. He felt intense pain, tasted blood and thought; "these guys are going to kill me."

He heard, "How do you like that you fucking Indian? I thought you Indians were supposed to be so tough."

The guy who pulled his hands away from his face was holding Hap's arms down as another stomped on his fingers.

"Let's kill the dirty, fucking Indian", someone said. They continued to kick Hap in the head and face while some stomped on him. Hap thought, "I can't pass out or they are going to kill me."

"He's done," one of them said." Let's drag him over the snow bank and throw him in the ditch."

The last thing Hap thought was, "this is it" – as he felt himself being dragged over the snow bank and rolled down into the ditch.

POMMELED

I am beaten, squashed again
not by physical force or even a blow
but by the pompous strike of authority
pommeling my senses and self worth to nil
feelings of shame, always in the wrong.
Why does this have to be?
Am I not a person?
Who hast died and made him King
or is it all in my mind
programmed to subservience
by One who has no more power than I?

A NEW DAY

A light pinkish tinge, colors the morning sky
It washes across the heavens, like dawn's fading night
Shimmering light dances over the waters
Morning dew glistens the grasses
Mother Earth's lifeblood flows over rocks
Rainbows appear as spectrums in the mists
Revealing mystical fountains as dawn awakens
She opens dark canyons as shadows echo a path
Along rocky outcrops and fields of blue
All for the wondrous amazement
of me and you.

WHAT WILL YOU DO?

In times of pain and sorrow
In times of indecision and questions
In times of injustice and racism
Instead of doing nothing
Do peace

In times of heartbreak and grief
In times of wondering and disbelief
In times of courage and valor
Do as Martin Luther King did
Do peace

In times of defeat and surrender
In times of failure and loss
In times of unbearable pain
Recall the wisdom of Chief Joseph
Do peace

In times of indifference and apathy
In times of total surrender
In times of coldness and despair
Emulate the patience of Mother Teresa
Do peace

In times of seeking to make a difference
In times of wondering what can I do
In times of a call to action
In times of doing the right thing
Do peace

As I seek to achieve humility
I daily ask the Creator for strength
To recall these simple words
Today in my life I will
Do peace

GRANDMA'S

The butterflies have started their dance
my mind once an ally is now an unrelenting foe
have the early morning runs and miles paid off
or is it all a foolish dream and wishful thought

race morning is here I try to act calm
but the questions still linger in my mind
the excitement, music and all the people
gives one an adrenalized rush to proceed

helicopters and media make it a surreal event
the starting gun and the mass start is off
no longer alone, but with thousands who soar
so far nothing compares to this

as the miles go by I can't believe it's me
my training, friends advice and dreams pay off
I pass the twenty mile mark and run on
my doubts turn to belief

the crowds on the way energize my wings
my body is learning to fly
under the Lake Avenue bridge
as the crowd goes wild

tears of joy and pain flow with the sweat
I hear my name and cry out with ecstasy
I have joined the ranks of Phidippedes
And victory is mine

A mere mortal who has finished
The Grandma's Marathon

YOUR LOVE

At night alone, I think of your love and feel mistrust
all your promises of love, are as worthless as dust

I see all your failures and deceit as I cry
the tears will not stop as I wonder why

Why you lie to me all the time
with each tale of woe you seem fine

Do you have a conscience or soul
or are you so twisted you do not know

All I know is I can't take anymore
because each day I fight a war

Of hearing you say, I love you
and wonder what's really true

Do you not respect me or think me a fool
and laugh at me because you are so cruel

I must be stupid and a complete idiot
to allow your abuse and not forget

Forget, that I truly do love you
but I cannot let you do as you do

So goodbye forever
because it will never be

Your love

ENDLESS NIGHT

I can't wait to get to sleep at night
trying so hard to make it right

I wake up too early in the dark
my mind can't slow my racing heart

seeking comfort to satisfy my soul
a spiritual release to reach that goal

lost in spirit, lost in time
lost in love and lost in mind

I feel so completely lost
searching for relief at any cost

I'm so sad what can make it right
a darkness that feels like everlasting night

IS THIS LOVE?

I'm back, to my never ending search
a dream unfulfilled, hope for a new start
I met a woman she captured my heart
my soul, my dreams and desires
a life spent together, a state of bliss
faults disappear with a loving kiss

I miss you, your touch, your laughter
your smile, your soft, gentle caress
I love you forever, always, please remember
true love never dies, it grows and grows
what bad memories linger, recall the good ones
it's sad you doubted my love for you

I tried so hard to have you believe
but the guilt and fault lies on me
what could have been different, I know not
my faults still haunt me, for answers still sought
I feel sorrow and longing, for the love that was lost
dreams and desires die hard, grief is the cost

I pray someday you will truly understand
when I said, I love you and offered my hand
it was from deep, within my soul
offering a part of me, I did not even know
I wish you listened to your heart, instead of your friends
which was truly the beginning of the end

Feelings of love, someone to care for and hold
hear my plea, of tears shed, uncontrolled
hope of daring to risk, eluded my past
it's a circle for me that cannot last
I need love, acceptance, strength to move on
to cease to mourn, for a love that is gone ...

NIGHTFALL

As night takes over
it envelopes the light in a soft cocoon
shading a red sky as it slowly disappears
dusk pulls twilight into a sleepy dream
stars appear as sparkling, silver-like crystal
dark of night accentuates a primal sense
glittering moonlight reflects over the dark waters
clouds sail by as waves swish across the rocks
a single moonbeam points to a rising silver orb
the bewitching hour has begun
one falls under a magic spell
as night takes over

WANNABE

Sometimes I meet people who say
they wish they were Indian
or you're lucky to be an Indian
or there's Indian in their blood or family

Would they still say that
if they knew what names we were called
such as: drunken Indian, dirty Indian, crazy Comanche
war whoop, wagon burner, squaw man and Injun man

Better yet, they claim to honor us
by names such as: chief, warrior, brave and redskin
they wear war paint, mock sacred ceremonies
do the tomahawk chop and mimic war dances

They say we don't have to pay taxes
get free medical, free college tuition, big casino profits
monthly checks, can hunt and fish with no limit
anytime and anyplace we want

Who wouldn't want to be an Indian
I wish I was an Indian

FIRST TRI

"What the hell am I doing here?" I said.

I found myself at the start of a sprint triathlon on a hot, August summer day. I had never swam any distance other than laps in junior high school, which had seemed to be an awfully, long time ago. Well, here I was nervous, scared and asking myself, "What the hell am I doing here?"

My friend, Lyle, had asked me to act as a safety lookout for him, as he swam in preparation for this triathlon. After watching Lyle swim and finding out the distance was, "only a 600 yard swim," I had foolishly registered. I now wondered if I had a momentary lapse of reason.

I had some success in running and considered myself a better than average biker. My only worry was the swim, which I figured I could breast stroke, side stroke or even dog paddle if I had to. I watched the others warming up with a swim. I thought, "Those guys must be crazy! Wasting all that energy swimming, they're nuts. I'm smarter than that," or so I thought. "I will just play it cool and relax." One thing that bothered me was that the buoys marking the 600 yard swim looked pretty damn far away! I was sure that they were a lot further away than 600 yards.

I looked around at all the other triathletes with all their fancy gear: wetsuits, speedos, tri-bikes and racing tri-uniforms. Those guys looked to be pretty serious. I suddenly felt like a fool and wanted to go home. But I had paid my entry fee so I might as well give it a try. I relaxed a little and saw some people I recognized from the running circuit. They were friendly, exchanged pleasantries and told me to have a good race. Some even commented to me, "Doug, I didn't know you were a triathlete?"

I said, "I'm not, this is my first one'."

They replied, "Cool, have fun!"

Maybe this was going to be okay, after all. I walked down to the lake like everybody else and thought, "Wow, I am in my first triathlon." The excitement was contagious and helped calm my nerves. It was exciting, just like a running race and I was anxious to start. Once the swim started, I was really nervous again and for good reason, too. Everybody around me looked like they were really, good swimmers. I started in the back of the pack, probably swam out around fifty feet or so and started to tread water. I was sure glad I remembered that basic skill.

Soon, the women's wave caught up with me and swam over top of me as I desperately tried to get out of their way. I started to panic and tried to get inside next to the floats. I was getting hit and kicked by the other swimmers as they swam by. I was in trouble as I felt myself sinking and my arms felt like lead weights. I flailed to stay afloat, pin-wheeling my arms and knocked my goggles sideways which immediately filled with water! I inhaled a mouthful of water and started to cough and choke. I thought I was going to drown and have to ask for rescue assistance.

My friend, Matt, saw me struggling and asked me if I was okay. This calmed me somewhat, as I told him yes, but wondered if I really was. A women rescuer on a surfboard asked me if I needed to rest. I said okay, but I did not want to get disqualified. She said I was fine as long as I only rested once and was able to continue on my own.

The rest re-energized me as I thought, "I can really do this." Then, the only problem I had was the cheap goggles I was using kept filling up with water. I finally pulled them off and just threw them. I was slow, alternating with the breast stroke and side stroke but after I rounded the first buoy marker, I was getting confident on finishing the swim and not getting disqualified. I was going to finish the swim.

As I emerged from the water I thanked the Creator for getting me through the swim and now would be on familiar ground. The transition from swim to bike was slow but a real eye opener. I stepped on my towel, wiped my feet, put on my shoes and grabbed my helmet. I put on my helmet, remembering to clip it before taking my bike off the rack. Too late, I forgot to put on my shirt. I tried to pull it on over my helmet to save time, but that was not going to work. So off with my helmet and on with my shirt, now I was ready to go. "Oh shoot", I said as I forgot my sunglasses. I looked around frantically, where were they?

Wasting more time! I was ready to go without them as I spied them lying on my towel. I quickly put them on and was finally off on my bike. The bike leg was smooth as I passed people all the way and I was on a mountain bike! I felt a little cocky as I passed a number of high performance tri-bikes. I thought maybe I was going too hard, but passing all the high tech bikes acted as a stimulant.

The sun was out in full force so I took in water from the bottle on my bike. Every ten to fifteen minutes like everyone had said; a smart move and very important strategy. The 10 mile bike went by fast and soon I was rounding the comer into transition two, bike to run. I felt like I may have gone too hard on the bike but, oh well, too late now. I stepped off my bike and I was on rubber Leg Street. I almost lost my balance as I used my bike to steady myself to keep from falling. I thought, "Oh no, I'm never going to be able to finish the run." I found my spot and put my bike on the rack. I took off my helmet and my sunglasses went flying. I had put them on over my helmet strap. Oh well, here we go again. Someone was kind enough to pick them up for me and said, "Here, you might need these." I laughed, said thank you and knew I was going to be okay.

I took off on the run and my legs felt big and heavy, like two lead balloons. I remembered to relax and go slow and forget about speed. I did and it worked. Soon, I was able to pick up my speed and I felt stronger. I was passing quite a few people which had a synergistic effect on me to push even harder. One mile went by, then the turn around and I was over half way done. The run was my strong point so I excelled. Since this was a sprint triathlon, the run was only three miles. The last half mile went by and I actually felt good. As I rounded the last turn into the finish chute the crowd was cheering. I was ecstatic as I realized I was going to cross the finish line! I felt like a winner. I had just finished a triathlon; I was now, a real- triathlete!

Authors note: Safety first. I did possess a water safety certificate prior to the event but nothing replaces adequate training with a tri team, especially for beginners.

ZIIGWAAN

I love a run, on a warm, spring day
along a well worn path through the woods
beside a stream
that calls with a sweet, soft sound
water gently flowing over rocks
cascading downhill
after a night of life giving, warm gentle rain
birch buds blossom, popple scents burst with aroma
lilacs, wildflowers and damp earth permeate the air
morning dew dissipates, as swirling mists take flight
shimmering heat waves dance above the ground
songbirds call out their cheerful melodies
the sights, the sounds, the intoxicating fresh smells
create a moment of indescribable peace
a oneness of nature and self
feeling this is the way it should be
the love of Mother Earth, Creator and self

WISDOM

Where have all the years gone
It was only yesterday when I was a teen
and everyone over thirty was old
now I have gray in my hair, age lines on my face
wisdom from experience, not from being old
though I still do not possess the knowledge of my elders
I can show my respect
for their love in guiding my path, lifting my spirit
listening to teaching me their ways
showing I do not know it all

MANIDOO

A sanctuary that is sacred to the people
a place where you can communicate with the spirits
to enjoy the quiet solitude of nature's song
no traffic, no city noise -just peaceful bliss
escape to a forgotten time and place
to be with my spirit in a peaceful world
a time of spirit prayers, communication with the animals
answers come as the spirits reply
an eagle appears to circle above
hawks call and cry out their presence
the trees, grasses, wind and waters are alive
this sacred place exists within our prayers
Spirit Mountain

NIIBIN

The sun sets in a fiery red sky
waves softly lap against the shore
a warm breeze blows across the land
the haunting song of a loon echoes over the water
wood smoke, pine and earth assail the senses
a beaver slaps her tail as she glides along
frogs and crickets add to the chorus of sounds
the fire crackles as smoke slowly curls up
like ghostly fingers clutching at thin air
as the light fades to dusk
who can deny
Manidoowaadizi
The spirits live here

X

Cry wolf and let loose the dogs of war
Use your hatred and anger to destroy me
It's the only way you feel you can even the score
Though your reasoning and logic are skewed
Likened to an addict needing a fix to get well
Will you ever sense the wrongfulness of your right
Or have your friends programmed your mind to fiction
to believe the stories you've conditioned yourself to accept
because the truth requires honesty and trust
something you are incapable of believing or giving
so you lose, I lose, we all lose
and the world is safe for you to play your game
because people are a game
for you to play
as you see fit

TECHNOPHOBIA

Domes and smooth glimmering metallic surfaces, dot the landscape
sunshine glints across the vast, shiny glass towers
the constant hum of power for the huge, monstrous computer banks
dazzles the senses
Machines do all routine tasks now
I have no life
except to wander aimlessly and exist.

COMING BACK TO LIFE

My spirit's been to hell and back
a road to nowhere on an endless track
the depths of despair, the cellar of hell
one thought only, who can ever tell

A cry for help that went unanswered
no relief from pain, that cannot be heard
until someone came along, willing to listen and care
no judgment, no blame, just comfort to be there

Hope rises, as unfounded fears take flight
distorted reality, no longer seems to be right
thanks for being a friend, who truly understands
to offer a kind word and extend a warm loving hand

I feel I am coming back to life
coming back to life, feeling free, flying high
no worry, no cares, and dreams awakened
sailing along with the sun's rays, soaring across the sky

My spirit soars with the wind, racing with the clouds
the sun's rays bounce off the mirrored water's surface
reflecting the carefree thoughts of disassociation
one with self, the world, the universe and beyond

How perfect can this be, its never done
loving life, endless bliss, existing as one
a wisp of light, over the clouds, across the sky
On wings untethered, spirit unleaden, soaring high

I feel I am coming back to life
coming back to life, feeling free, flying high
no worry, no cares, and dreams awakened
sailing along with the sun's rays, soaring across the sky

ENIGMA

The beginning, a rhythmic beat
the heartbeat of life, a delicate thread

Out of the darkness I came seeking light
there's too much beauty to quit

It's time to grab the reins
and guide your destiny

Open your eyes a little wider
don't go- you can't see what you're missing

Stay with me, please, stay with me
I don't know what's real anymore

I'm already dead, it's a fact I can accept
now I can function and live my life

Because we're all here for a short time
the real question is, can we deal with the question

Of us and them, as ordinary humans
without a thought of hate

It's never to late
to walk down the path of light

Instead of, into the dark

OFFERING

The day begins with an offering of tobacco
as the sun rises, dreams and hopes lift
smoke from the pipe carries the prayer to the Great Spirit
an eagle spirals upward to deliver the message
who am I to say-it is not so
does the belief hurt me in any way
as an Elder once told me
He offered tobacco everyday
I asked him, did it work
He replied, does it matter to you, if it works or not
as I have gained wisdom, I finally understand
the tradition of offering tobacco, everyday

DARK DISTRESS

They shuffle along the street
like zombies looking for a soul to steal
but it is they who have had their souls stolen,
their spirits trashed, by an evil as relentless as death.
Demons and spirits lie inside, dormant 'til summoned by fate
these images haunt these poor stricken souls.
Searching for an escape, some way out,
no one plans this future to be, it just happens
all have the same thought, not me...

RUNNING DRUG FREE

Running has saved my life and helped me recover from my addiction to drugs and alcohol. The new feelings I have experienced in my second chance in life are more fantastic than any high I have ever known before. What intensifies these feelings is to know this is reality; it is not some artificially induced feeling produced by some chemical. This is what life is, and for me, there is hope, where there was none before. Call it an addiction to running or whatever but it is a positive addiction. Nothing like the depressing existence I was living in before. I actually feel like I am worth something, not useless and deplorable. Running may not be the solution for everyone, but it is the best solution I have found. When I discovered drugs and alcohol as a teenager, I thought I had discovered something new: escape from life through the use of chemicals. This was something I destructively pursued for seventeen years. It would lead me numerous times to jails, institutions and nearly death. Three strikes and you're out. Well, I should have been out. Treatment centers, halfway houses, jails and detox centers were my home. Recovery programs did not seem to work for me; something always seemed to be missing. The best intentions invariably led back to using. I had tried to use running twice before as a supplement to a program of recovery, both times ending in failure. I felt doomed as one of such unfortunates. Spiritually broken, mentally, physically and emotionally bankrupt, I felt the time to end it all had arrived. As they say, this was it. I found myself in another correctional facility and finally realized there had to be a change.

The first step in recovery was to actually quit using drugs and alcohol. Then, to decide what I was going to do, now that the hazy fog of constant chemical abuse started to lift. The only thing I was sure of was that there had to be some kind of replacement for the drugs and alcohol. Running seemed like a possible solution because I remembered the good feeling I used to get after a hard, strenuous workout. I started with jogging a block, then walk one, then jog another. This continued to progress to a quarter mile, half mile and finally a mile. Within a couple of months, I was up to about five miles a day, four to five times a week. I kept at it because it was the only way I could deal with all the stress I was experiencing as a result of my chemical free life. I felt good though, good enough to continue with my running program. I was now running five miles non-stop about five to six days a week. My spirit and self- esteem was lifting. There was a feeling of accomplishment and success. Here was something I could do that I actually enjoyed doing, without using chemicals. It had seemed like a lifetime ago that I remembered enjoying myself. One more thing I discovered was that I could set goals. My goal was to run in a five mile race and finish. I also decided the cigarettes would have to go. Smoking and long distance running do not mix. I was taking steps to becoming a real runner. My first race was a five mile run. I wanted to finish and finish in about thirty-five minutes. That figures out to be about a seven minute per mile pace. Not too bad I thought. I finished in thirty-five minutes even. What a feeling! The people cheering; I could not get over it. I was so happy I felt like crying. This was something I wanted to continue. I felt respect for myself and thought if I kept training, I could run faster. Not only run faster, but to experience all the excitement surrounding a running race. This was positive, healthy fun and was just what I needed. Maybe some day I might even win a trophy but that was dreaming. I was far from winning a trophy but it was a great motivational tool. The feelings of general depression were gone. Thoughts of suicide as a solution or wondering if it all is worthwhile were replaced by positive thoughts and feelings. I am not a prisoner to the disease of addiction today.

Some other interesting, unexpected changes have come about as well. My trust and belief in people has become a reality. I used to hate everybody, especially myself. This has changed to believing I am worth something and people are not all bad. One of the greatest rewards from this new life is the fact that I can affect other people in a positive sense. The people I have met have been great and they help me to continue in what I am doing. New friends and associates tell me of the respect and admiration they have for me. This has a synergistic effect on me and enables me to push for more. These are some of the gifts I have received from my new life of being drug and alcohol free. What started out as a way to deal with all the pressures of quitting the use of chemicals, has turned into a major focus in my life. Seven years of running and racing has been good to me. I have completed over a dozen marathons with a personal best at Grandma's Marathon of two hours and fifty one minutes, Twin Cities Marathon finish of two hours and fifty six minutes and completion of a few ultra marathons are some of my accomplishments. One year I was named most improved runner of the year by the Northern Minnesota Track Club along with setting a state record in a fifty-kilometer road race. I finished third overall in The Death Valley Trail Marathon a few years back and have won races from one to ten miles. I now have numerous trophies and awards in one to fifty miles which shows that I am a real runner. To be considered a good runner is something I never dreamed would be a reality, but this is my life today and I love it.

I have been asked to speak to youth groups, high school teams and people in alcohol and drug treatment about my experiences with drugs, alcohol and running. This helps me to stay honest, focused about myself and to help others. Inspiring others through sharing my personal story is a spiritual reward. I feel I am a productive member of society, no longer a detriment. Life is something to enjoy not something to endure. Even though it's not all hearts and flowers, it is much better than before. I am learning to accept life on life's terms. Today, I have a sense of hope for the future and dreams to pursue.

College writing 101, spring 1992

45

WALK A MILE IN MY MOCCASINS

I was born an Ojibwe Indian child, adopted by a loving white couple who wanted a son.

The circumstances surrounding my adoption are not to blame, it just happened. I was four years old and lived in a small northern Minnesota town.

My younger years were pretty much normal. I remember my Dad telling me I would probably have to fight but do not start it. I should just make sure I stood up for myself. I had friends and I knew I was Ojibwe but it really did not make any difference. The town was small enough so most people knew my story and I was accepted.

My only recollection of problems was when our little school participated in activities that were held at the big school in town. I remember being called names such as injun, chief, squaw man and redskin. I did not like it when we had to go to town to the school but, even at the young age of eight, I knew all people were not that ignorant.

We moved to Duluth when I was ten years old. It was the middle of fifth grade for me during Christmas break. I was a new student, obviously Ojibwe, attending a middle class school where I was the only Native American student there. The first few days were okay, a couple of the neighborhood kids were friendly with me. The relatives I was staying with had some kids who were known to the neighbors as "okay kids." This helped me some but people questioned how I was related to them.

The first day in gym class was a disaster. Since we had moved rather suddenly I did not have any tennis shoes which were required in the gym.

I had to participate in gym class in my bare feet while everyone else had tennis shoes. All the other kids, with the exception of a few, thought this was hilarious. They laughed at me and made jokes about my family being poor because I didn't have tennis shoes. They threw pennies at me and called me names. This was the beginning of the worst time in my life. I thought the teasing, name calling and being made fun of would quit after they got to know me, but I was wrong. It continued to get worse when I ignored them. It seemed like I was always getting it from somewhere or someone.

I ended up getting into a fight with one of the kids who was thought to be one of the toughest guys in school.

I didn't want to fight or get into trouble but I had no choice. The other kid shoved me into the lockers really hard. Then he grabbed me. I fought back when a teacher happened to walk by. I got blamed for starting the fight and had to go to the principal's office. The teasing and fights continued for the rest of the year. I was known as an easy target to start trouble with at school.

The kids picked out a new name for me because I liked milk and I once drank three other kids' chocolate milk. The kids laughed at me for drinking all that milk.

They said, "Hey, he's chocolate colored and likes chocolate milk, let's call him Choco."

I did not say anything because I thought if I did not say anything, they would quit. They took my silence as being agreeable to that derogatory name.

One boy said, "Yea, you like that name don't you, Choco?"

I didn't say anything.

He said, "See, I told you he likes it, right, Choco?"

I hated that name but I knew what happened when I stood up for myself. In the mornings before the teacher would come into the classroom, someone would start a sing-song phrase about that name. Something like "Choco, Choco likes tacos, because he's so poor, that's all his family can afford." I would get mad and give it back to them and would get blamed for starting fights. I quit saying anything about it.

It seemed like I was always getting into some kind of trouble; like stealing, destroying personal belongings, fights and general misbehavior.

Other students would take something from someone, then put it in my desk and tell the teacher they saw me take their stuff. The teacher would check my desk and find the stolen property. Then, I would be sent to the office. I was scared to death because I had never been sent to the office before and did not know what was going to happen.

The counselor would have me read books, and then say, "You seem like a smart, nice boy, why do you do these things to cause trouble? Don't you like your classmates?"

I tried to explain all the teasing and things the other students were doing but he obviously did not believe me.

These types of things happened more frequently as the school year progressed.

I remember one day another kid was "popping" milk cartons while the teacher was out of the room. He popped a few and kicked them over by me. I was standing there watching and laughing. The teacher walked in just as the other kid popped another milk carton and I was laughing wholeheartedly. I was not the only kid standing there laughing, but I was the one who was grabbed by the arm as the teacher yelled at me for being a clown. The teacher said I could laugh my way to the principal's office as he roughly grabbed me and continued to shove me down the hall. He kept yelling at me asking, "How funny is it now, wise guy?"

I was too scared and shaking to answer because I really thought he was going to hit me. When I got back to class, the other kids were laughing about what happened They commented on how funny it was when the teacher grabbed me and was yelling at me.

They would say, "Happy got sent to the office again, hah, hah, hah. Are you going to get suspended?"

This seemed to be a never-ending story about me causing trouble. I hoped this nonsense would end soon but it got worse and worse.

The last day of school was supposed to be a fun, easy day and all the kids were excited, especially me. During the last hour of the day, the science teacher said we could have free time and I wanted to draw. Some girl told the teacher I was bothering her. I was not but when she walked by to go up to the teacher, I sensed something was wrong.

The teacher, Mrs.Coalmen said, "Happy, come up here, Sue told me you were bothering her. I should have known, the last day of school and you can't even behave yourself. Guess who gets to stay after school."

I said, "I wasn't doing anything. I ride the bus. What am I supposed to do?"

Coalmen snorted, "That's tough, you should have thought about that before you started bothering Sue. I don't care what you do, but you are staying after school today."

I knew better than to protest or deny the lie Sue had made up so I just said, "Okay."

My heart sank and I felt like I had been hit in the stomach. I wanted to scream and cry but wouldn't give anyone the pleasure of seeing me hurt so I just remained silent.

I had missed the bus so I ended up walking home.

A few blocks from the school I saw this bigger kid in the sixth grade who didn't like me.

I said, "Hi."

He said, "Choco, what are you doing in my neighborhood, did I say you can be here?"

He punched me in the stomach and threw me down in the ditch.

I had the wind knocked out of me and was too stunned to do anything. He grabbed me by the arm twisting it, he said, "Come on, I know some guys who want to see you. You know my cousin, Billy, and my brother?"

"I know some other guys who would love to know you're around our neighborhood. We're going to teach you to not be in our neighborhood."

He dragged me over to a house across the street and knocked on the door. A girl I recognized from my class answered and told him nobody else was around.

Rich said, "You're lucky, Choco, if Billy and those other guys were around, you wouldn't be walking home. If I ever see you in my neighborhood again I'm not going to be so easy on you."

He kicked me really hard in the rear end as I walked away. I just wanted to be away from that school and those kids.

We moved down to the Central Hillside of Duluth and even though I was the new kid again, it was nothing like before. I made friends right away like I usually did and things seemed to be okay. When school started there were Blacks, Asians and other Indians. I felt relieved. I did not get into many fights or have any of the problems I had at that other school. School was fun again and I had friends.

When I started at Washington Junior High School, a lot of the kids from the school I was at in fifth grade were there, too. It didn't take too long and some of the same things started up again. Some of the kids remembered me and must have thought they could do the same things to me again. I did my best to avoid fights but I was getting sick and tired of the other kid's nonsense. This went on for most of seventh grade but as the year ended, I couldn't take it anymore.

One certain boy wanted to fight me. He kept pushing me and punching me in the back. One day, while I was walking down the hallway, he kicked me in the rear end and called me a name. I had enough I turned around and punched him in the face as hard as I could.

He said, "Come on, Happy, let's go in the bathroom and finish it."

I gladly took him up on his offer. We went in the second floor washroom and fought. A large number of kids watched as I ended up beating the daylights out of him. One of his friends tried to fight me just as I finished with his friend.. The end result was the same. I punched him in the face and head about five or six times. He decided he had enough and was in tears. He tried to blame the fight on me after going to the assistant principal with a bullshit story. The assistant principal did not believe him and I was not in trouble.

This started my reputation as a fighter and tough kid. I got in a few more fights that year and came out on top. The days of getting picked on and pushed around were over. I told myself what had happened before was not going to happen again. I did not start fights but I didn't take any flak, either. I don't condone violence but I will stick up for myself.

Today, I am a long distance runner who trains out on the streets of Duluth. I do not take unnecessary chances or get in the way of cars but the drivers think I do. Most people wave or toot the horn. Some have cursed me out, shouted racial slurs and tried to run me off the road. People have actually turned around in their cars and come back to threaten what they are going to do to me. This is a perfect example of where I won't back down.

Some times it feels like fifth grade, all over again.

CODE OF ARROGANCE

Sometimes a person knows what they know
especially about themselves and their downfalls

Who are you to say different
do you live in my mind, body or spirit?

Does a degree, or letters after your name
mean you possess-superior knowledge

To make decisions, to ruin somebody's life
with swiftness, that cuts like a knife

Above the lowly souls you reign
because of letters after your name

Do you have a conscience or soul?
or are you so insolent, that's unknown

Corrections counselor title, grants a manifesto
to relish grandiose power with pomp gusto

To admit fault is against the code
the contemptuousness a heavy load

Although repentance is nil
I pray for thy will

REMEMBRANCE

How can you measure unconditional love?
Which surely must be, a gift from above?

Not in amount and definitely not in time
We all have borrowed moments, lest we be blind

There's a hole in my soul I can't relieve
Intense pain, deep inside-beyond belief

That you're gone it can't be so
Every fiber of my being cries out no

Before your time my friend, you're gone
I cry at night into the early dawn

How honored I was, to have you as my friend
When love is forever how can your time ever end

I love you so much, where does it go
My love will be forever, entwined in my soul

The day you left it rained and set you free
Mother Earth cried as it was meant to be

I miss you so much but I'll see you again
Because that hope keeps me going, until then

When we meet in spirit, the circle will be complete
And our love for each other be forever sweet

SPIRIT OF THE LAND

They stand watch, invisible specters-justice untried
Scanning the lands they held, lost and died
Their blood flowed with the tears they cried
Mourning their loss with pain deep inside

Oh how they pray for the days of old
Connection of nature worth more than gold
Stories from the elders need to be told
Respect for Mother Earth cannot be sold

The ancestors fought to hold these things dear
Treaty rights, hunting and gathering honored, without fear
The great white father made these promises clear
But treaties broken with none shedding a tear

We have come full circle, casino profits are power
Their want of hunting and fishing grow stronger by the hour
What can they take next, things look to be dour
The spirit is the answer to empower

Some things cannot be explained but do exist
A feeling inside, one with creation, nothing amiss
A sense of harmony, a fleeting wisp
As the spirits merge, as one with the mist

ABOUT THE AUTHOR

Doug Happy's stories and poems reflect a lifetime of personal experiences. His work is influenced by the natural environment of northern Minnesota as well as by the people who live in the region. A frequent contributor to local publications, this is his first book.

A graduate of the College of St. Scholastica in Duluth, Minn., Doug is a long-time advocate of those who are less fortunate in this world. He currently works as a homeless shelter coordinator serving hundreds of people in need each year.

Doug is a well-known athlete not only in Duluth but throughout the region and is a talented and skilled runner. He is frequently seen training on the roads and streets in Duluth. In recent years, he has taken up triathlon racing adding the elements of swimming and biking to his already exceptional running. He has an appetite for adventure having fought fires in the western United States and loves black diamond and extreme ski runs in the Rocky Mountains of Colorado.

With an interest in drama and acting, Doug has performed in many local theater productions and was a member of the cast of "Chasing Indigo," an independent movie filmed in the Duluth area in 1998. He was also in the feature film *North Country* filmed on the Iron Range of Minnesota.

Doug Happy currently lives in northeastern Minnesota and is a member of the Mille Lacs Band of Ojibwe.

Authors note: I have included a copy of my court record to show my stories are true and not embellished from my past.

CRH

SIP-NO: 0008917   HAPPY DOUGLAS WILLIAM   DOB: 040558

```
RN  DATE   JUDGE      CASE      OFFENSE                    NOTES
)01 041276 WILSON     26069     103 -ASSAULT
)02 080276 WILSON     30154     101 -DISORDERLY CONDUCT
)03 020277 BUJOLD     35680     103 -ASSAULT
)04 020277 BUJOLD     35681     110 -RESISTING ARREST
)05 081677 ABELSON    42721     101 -DISORDERLY CONDUCT
)06 081677 ABELSON    42722     110 -RESISTING ARREST
)07 081677 ABELSON    42723     103 -ASSAULT
)08 100377 WILSON     44862     003 -DWI
)09 011981 WILSON     97334     101 -DISORDERLY CONDUCT   D.M.C.A.
)10 011981 WILSON     97335     103 -ASSAULT              G. 10 CJ, STAYED
                                                          VICTIM-
)11 042881 WILSON     102144    122 -ASSAULT POLICE OFFIC DMCA
)12 042881 WILSON     102145    101 -DISORDERLY CONDUCT   PB30CJ CR TIMESERVED
)13 052781 SWEENEY    8101678   107 -TRESPASS             DMCA
)14 052881 SWEENEY    8101679   103 -ASSAULT              G60CJ 8-6MOS PROB
                                                          VICTIM-
)15 060878 BUJOLD     53185     101 -DISORDERLY CONDUCT   PG 20CJ S-SUSPENDED
        PF1 KEY TO PAGE FORWARD
                 HIT ENTER TO CONTINUE
CRH
```

SIP-NO: 0008917   HAPPY DOUGLAS WILLIAM   DOB: 040558

```
RN  DATE   JUDGE      CASE      OFFENSE                    NOTES
)16 011079 WILSON     56918     135 -VIOLATION OF PROBATI REVOKED SERVE 42CJ
)17 112778 WILSON     59955     177 -URINATE IN PUBLIC     G $25
)18 011079 WILSON     63214     101 -DISORDERLY CONDUCT    G 42CJ
    201202 SWEENEY    8201676   10A -THEFT (FRAUD)         20CJ CR. TIME SERVED
```

58

```
021 051479 SWEENEY    8354C    107 -TRESPASS          PG C30
022 050482 BUJOLD     8204113  197 -MISC CRIMINAL     PG$30 SS
023 040282 BUJOLD     8204114  229 -ARSON             DC4-12-82 B5000 C
024 070682 WILSON     8208332  103 -ASSAULT           G 30CJ PROB 6MTHS
                                                      VIC-*
025 072182 WILSON     8209024  101 -DISORDERLY CONDUCT G, NO SENTENCE
026 072182 WILSON     8209025  103 -ASSAULT           G 60CJ
                                                      VICTIM-*
027 030483 MURPHY     8303060  103 -ASSAULT           G 90CJ
                                                      VIC.
028 030483 MURPHY     8303061  110 -RESISTING ARREST  DMCA
029 030483 MURPHY     8303062  101 -DISORDERLY CONDUCT DMCA
        PF1 KEY TO PAGE FORWARD      PF2 KEY TO PAGE BACK
                 HIT ENTER TO CONTINUE

NCRH

   SIP-NO: 0008917   HAPPY DOUGLAS WILLIAM            DOB: 040558

                                                       NOTES
TRN DATE   JUDGE     CASE     OFFENSE                G30CJNOS/C
030 092683 BUJOLD    8314049  101 -DISORDERLY CONDUCT (SHOPLIFTING)ADMITS
031 062184 BUJOLD    8317186  135 -VIOLATION OF PROBATI PROB REV-COMMIT TO
                                                      NERCC
032 020984 OSWALD    8317187  101 -DISORDERLY CONDUCT DMCA
033 062184 BUJOLD    8317188  135 -VIOLATION OF PROBATI CRMDMGTOPROP-ADMITS
                                                      PROB REVOKED-COMMIT.
                                                      TO NERCC
034 020984 OSWALD    8400584  101 -DISORDERLY CONDUCT DMCA
035 062184 BUJOLD    8400585  135 -VIOLATION OF PROBATI RESIST ARREST-ADMITS
                                                      PROB REV COMMIT TO
                                                      NERCC
036 062184 BUJOLD    8408665  101 -DISORDERLY CONDUCT PG 9CJ CREDIT FOR
                                                      TIME SERVED
                                                      COMMIT
037 021484 OSWALD    8317186  102 -SHOPLIFTING       G 90CJTOSERVE15DBAL
                                                      ON1YRPROB(B.KERNAN)

        PF1 KEY TO PAGE FORWARD      PF2 KEY TO PAGE BACK
                 HIT ENTER TO CONTINUE
NCRH
   SIP-NO: 0008917   HAPPY DOUGLAS WILLIAM            DOB: 040558

                                                       NOTES
TRN DATE   JUDGE     CASE     OFFENSE                G90CJTOSERVE15DBALON
038 020784 OSWALD    8400585  110 -RESISTING ARREST  1YRPROB(KERNAN)
039 022484 OSWALD    8317188  114 -CRIMINAL DAMAGE TO P G90CJTOSERVE15DBALON
                                                      PROB1YR(KERNAN)
040 061885 NORD      8506693  102 -SHOPLIFTING       DISMISSED BY COURT
041 090685 OSWALD    8507406  101 -DISORDERLY CONDUCT DMCA
042 090685 OSWALD    8508318  101 -DISORDERLY CONDUCT PG 20CJ COMMITTED
043 090685 OSWALD    8510363  103 -ASSAULT           PG 20CJ NO S/C SS
                                                      VICTIM-*
044 090685 OSWALD    8510364  101 -DISORDERLY CONDUCT DMCA
045 090685 OSWALD    8511197  101 -DISORDERLY CONDUCT PG 20CJ NO S/C SS
    031286 OSWALD    8601455  0103-ASSAULT           G.30 CJ. SERVE CONS.
                                                      W/8601454,8602117 &
                                                      8601455. S COMM TO
                                                      3-14-86, 5:00P.M.


        PF1 KEY TO PAGE FORWARD      PF2 KEY TO PAGE BACK
                 HIT ENTER TO CONTINUE
NCRH
   SIP-NO: 0008917   HAPPY DOUGLAS WILLIAM            DOB: 040558
```

```
    SIP-NO: 0008917    HAPPY DOUGLAS WILLIAM              DOB: 040558

TRN  DATE   JUDGE        CASE       OFFENSE                       NOTES
     012088 OSWALD       8735113    0101-DISORDERLY CONDUCT   DISMISSED MOTION OF
                                                             CITY ATTORNEY
     012088 OSWALD       8735925    0101-DISORDERLY CONDUCT   DISMISSED MOTION OF
                                                             CITY ATTORNEY
     012088 OSWALD       8735923    0103-ASSAULT             PG 90 DAYS CJ- TO
                                                             SERVE 60 DAYS - BAL
                                                             ON 2 YRS PROB. CR.
                                                             FOR 35 DAYS SERVED
                                                             030388-COMM ON VIOL
                                                             PROB
     012088 OSWALD       8735924    0103-ASSAULT             DISMISSED MOTION OF
                                                             CITY ATTORNEY
     012088 OSWALD       8736043    0101-DISORDERLY CONDUCT  DISMISSED MOTION OF
                                                             CITY ATTORNEY
     012088 OSWALD       8736883    0101-DISORDERLY CONDUCT  DISMISSED MOTION OF
                                                             CITY ATTORNEY

       PF1 KEY TO PAGE FORWARD         PF2 KEY TO PAGE BACK
              HIT ENTER TO CONTINUE
```

```
    SIP-NO: 0008917    HAPPY DOUGLAS WILLIAM              DOB: 040558

TRN  DATE   JUDGE        CASE       OFFENSE                       NOTES
     012088 OSWALD       8736884    0103-ASSAULT             PG 90 DAYS CJ- STAY
                                                             ON 2 YRS PROB CONS W
                                                             8735923, 8737715 &
                                                             8800627    030388 -
     012088 OSWALD       8737715    0211-THEFT               COMM ON VIOL OF PROB
                                                             PG  90 DAYS CJ- STAY
                                                             2 YRS PROB CONS W/
                                                             8735923, 8736884 &
                                                             8800627    030388 -
                                                             DEF COMM ON VIOL OF
     012088 OSWALD       8738026    0101-DISORDERLY CONDUCT  PROB
                                                             DISMISSED MOTION OF
     012088 OSWALD       8800626    0211-THEFT               CITY ATTORNEY
                                                             DISMISSED MOTION OF
                                                             CITY ATTORNEY

       PF1 KEY TO PAGE FORWARD         PF2 KEY TO PAGE BACK
              HIT ENTER TO CONTINUE
```

```
    SIP-NO: 0008917    HAPPY DOUGLAS WILLIAM              DOB: 040558

TRN  DATE   JUDGE        CASE       OFFENSE                       NOTES
     012088 OSWALD       8800627    0103-ASSAULT             PG 90 DAYS CJ -
                                                             030388 - VIOL OF
                                                             PROB ADMITTED, STAY
                                                             REV, COMM CONS W/
                                                             8735923, #8736884,
     040588 OSWALD       8800904    0229-ARSON               #8737715
                                                             DISMISSED MOTION OF
     040588 OSWALD       8800905 B  0114-CRIMINAL DAMAGE TO P CITY ATTORNEY DISMISSED MOTION OF
     040588 OSWALD       8800905 A  0101-DISORDERLY CONDUCT  CITY ATTORNEY
                                                             PG 30 DAYS NERCC- C
                                                             CONCURRENT WITH TIME
```

60

TRN DATE	JUDGE	CASE	OFFENSE	NOTES
031286	OSWALD	8601454	0101-DISORDERLY CONDUCT	6.30 CJ. SERVE CONS. W/8601455, 8602117 & 8603777. S COMM TO 3-14-86, 5:00P.M.
031286	OSWALD	8601456	0103-ASSAULT	DISMISSED ON MOTION OF CITY ATTY.
031286	OSWALD	8602117	0101-DISORDERLY CONDUCT	6.30 CJ. SERVE CONS. W/8602777, 8601454 & 8601455. 6 COM TO 3-14-86, 5:00P.M.
031286	OSWALD	8603775	0101-DISORDERLY CONDUCT	DISMISSED ON MOTION OF CITY ATTY.
031286	OSWALD	8603777	0110-RESISTING ARREST	6.90 CJ. CONSECUTIVE W/8601454, 8601455 & 8602117. S COMM TO 3-14-86, 5:00PM
031286	OSWALD	8603776	0103-ASSAULT	DISMISSED ON MOTION

PF1 KEY TO PAGE FORWARD   PF2 KEY TO PAGE BACK
HIT ENTER TO CONTINUE

NCRH

SIP-NO: 0008917   HAPPY DOUGLAS WILLIAM   DOB: 040558

TRN DATE	JUDGE	CASE	OFFENSE	NOTES
031286	OSWALD	8603776	0103-ASSAULT	DISMISSED ON MOTION OF CITY ATTY.
110586	WILSON	8615414 A	0103-ASSAULT	PG - 60 DAYS CJ- CR FOR 10 DAYS SERVED- BAL ON 1 YR PROB-MS 062287 VIOL ADMITTED PROB REVOKED, COMM 062587 TO SERVE TIME
110586	WILSON	8615662	0101-DISORDERLY CONDUCT	DISMISSED MOTION OF CITY ATTORNEY
110586	WILSON	8615663	0107-TRESPASS	DISMISSED MOTION OF CITY ATTORNEY
110586	WILSON	8615664 B	0103-ASSAULT	PG 60 DAYS CJ- CR FOR 10 DAYS SERVED- BAL ON 1 YR PROB -MS CONSEC W/8615414, 062287 PROB REVOKED,

PF1 KEY TO PAGE FORWARD   PF2 KEY TO PAGE BACK
HIT ENTER TO CONTINUE

NCRH

SIP-NO: 0008917   HAPPY DOUGLAS WILLIAM   DOB: 040558

TRN DATE	JUDGE	CASE	OFFENSE	NOTES
110586	WILSON	8615664 B	0103-ASSAULT	PG 60 DAYS CJ- CR FOR 10 DAYS SERVED- BAL ON 1 YR PROB -MS CONSEC W/8615414, 062287 PROB REVOKED, SEE UACT NOTES
062287	OSWALD	8615414 A	0135-VIOLATION OF PROBATI	VIOL ADMITTED, PROB REVOKED COMM 062587 TO SERVE BAL OF TIME CONSE W/ 8615664ADMITTED, PROB
062287	OSWALD	8615664 B	0135-VIOLATION OF PROBATI	REVOKED, TO SERVE BAL OF TIME CONSEC W/8615414, CREDIT 21 DAYS
012088	OSWALD	8735113	0101-DISORDERLY CONDUCT	DISMISSED MOTION OF

PF1 KEY TO PAGE FORWARD   PF2 KEY TO PAGE BACK

PF1 KEY TO PAGE FORWARD   PF2 KEY TO PAGE BACK
                    HIT ENTER TO CONTINUE
NCRH

SIP-NO: 0008917   HAPPY DOUGLAS WILLIAM   DOB: 040558

TRN DATE JUDGE   CASE   OFFENSE   NOTES
     030388 OSWALD   8736884 B 0135-VIOLATION OF PROBATI VIOL ADMITTED, DEF
                                                           COMM TO SERVE BAL OF
                                                           TIME
     030388 OSWALD   8737715 C 0135-VIOLATION OF PROBATI VIOL ADMITTED, DEF
                                                           COMM TO SERVE TIME
     030388 OSWALD   8735923 D 0135-VIOLATION OF PROBATI VIOL ADMITTED, DEF
                                                           COMM TO SERVE BAL OF
                                                           TIME CONSEC W/
                                                           8736884, 8737715,
                                                           8800627 - CRED TIME
001 052082 BARNES   15346   101 -DISORDERLY CONDU DUL   SERVED
                                                           90D CJ CR T RED CHG

    * * * END OF LIST * * *   PF2 KEY TO PAGE BACK
               HIT ENTER TO CONTINUE